WRITE TO MARKET

Chris Fox

ISBN:1523898399
ISBN-13:9781523898398

To Mr. Market, for teaching so many of us to make a living at this

Introduction

If you've read *5,000 Words Per Hour* or *Lifelong Writing Habit* you already know what to expect in this intro. I'm not going to spend fifty pages telling you all the things this book will do for you. I'm going to do it in one sentence. This book will teach you how to analyze the market, and to use that information to write a book that readers want.

Some of you are immediately skeptical. Others are grabbing pitchforks and torches. Writing to market has some nasty connotations, and we've all been taught that what it really means is that you're selling out. I'm here to tell you that absolutely is not the case. If you want to be a successful author, then you need to master your craft. You need to tell amazing stories. But the kind of story you choose to tell can dramatically affect your career as an author.

There are two methods of writing a book. One has a much, much, higher chance of success than the other. The first method is writing whatever story pops into your head. This might result in you writing something new and unique, something that takes off like Harry Potter. Most likely it will result in you writing a book that almost no one reads. Harsh, but accurate.

The other method is contentious in the writing world. Many authors demonize this method, though I suspect very few really understand how or why it works. The second method is writing to market. The very term upsets people, because it's bandied about with no real understanding of what it means. Writing to market is *not* copying Hunger Games and changing a few names and places. Hundreds of authors attempted to do exactly that, and the vast majority of their books failed.

So what is it?

Writing to market is picking an underserved genre that you know has a voracious appetite, and then giving that market exactly what it wants. It means that before you write word one of your novel you already know you're going to have fans waiting to buy it. That may seem impossible, but trust me when I say it is absolutely achievable.

How do I know? Because I've utilized both methods. The first method served me fairly well, initially. My first novel was called *No Such Thing As Werewolves*. It turned several genres on their heads, and was very unique. Readers responded favorably, and the series continues to be my top seller.

So if the method was working, then why change it? Why start writing to market? Because I later realized that I'd *accidentally* written NSTAW to market. That wasn't clear until I attempted my first spin off.

I launched a second series called *Hero Born* that I touted as *X-Files* meets *Heroes*. I was immensely proud of it. It was unique and fun, and I assumed readers would love it. I had a large mailing list, an understanding of marketing and advertising, and a broad platform I used to launch the book.

The series sank like a rock, and the only people who bought it were loyal readers who loved my Deathless books. Everyone else ignored it, and three months later it still hasn't earned back what it cost to produce. If I followed the conventional wisdom offered in writing forums like Kboards I'd try to advertise the book. I'd try price pulsing. I'd mess with key words. Maybe I'd change the cover. I'd monkey with the blurb. You know what? I didn't do any of those things, because I understood *immediately* why the book failed.

I didn't write it to market. I wrote it, then *tried to market it.*

At the same time I launched *Hero Born* my friend Domino Finn launched a book called *Dead Man*. *Dead Man* was an urban fantasy written to market. It followed all the genre tropes, and is a slightly darker version of the *Dresden Files*. Fans loved it, and while my book sank, *Dead Man* took off. Nor was it the only book

I saw do that.

Dawn McKenna published a wonderful literary novel called *See You*. If you want a good cry, read the book. It's amazing. Very few people bought *See You*, and Dawn was in a rough financial spot. She decided to try something else. Dawn worked with powerhouse Wayne Stinnett, who all but owns the Sea Adventure genre. Dawn wrote a series to market, and went from two figures a month to hitting five figures a month.

R.M. Webb did the same thing. So did Cady Vance. The list of authors who transitioned into the writing to market model is long, and you'll hear more about them through the course of this book.

So I decided to do it too. My first attempt was a book many of you have read. *5,000 Words Per Hour* was written to market. I looked around at the non-fiction space, and realized there was room for another book on writing faster.

But this is the real rub, the thing many people get wrong. You can't just rehash a successful book. That way lies disaster. I didn't copy Rachel Aaron's *2k to 10k*. Instead, I figured out what problem she was solving, and solved the same problem in my own way. My book reads differently than others like it. It's shorter, more concise, and offers exercises at the end of every chapter. None of the others did that.

I hit the same tropes other successful books have hit, but I made sure to do it in my voice, and in my own way. If the idea of tropes is new, don't worry. I'll explain what they are, and how to analyze them for your genre. All you need to know right now is that before you start writing your next novel you need to understand the market you plan to aim it at.

So how about it? Have I piqued your interest? If so open up the book, and let's get cracking!

Chapter 1- Picking Your Market

Almost every time I hear the phrase write to market it's immediately followed by the words romance or erotica. That's hardly surprising, because those are by far the most widely read genres. A quick glance at the Amazon top 100 shows that a staggering 60 of the top books are in various romance subcategories. Even genres that have nothing to do with romance are littered with romance books.

Rest easy, though. I'm not here to tell you to write romance, unless you really enjoy writing romance. There are many other genres you can make a killing in, and odds are good at least one of them is an area you'd enjoy writing.

Writing to Market is Not Selling Out

Before we go any further I want to dispel one of the most damaging myths in our industry, the idea that writing to market is selling out. Quite frankly, that's B.S. If you write whatever you want to write and nothing else, then get ready to keep your day job forever.

If, on the other hand, you want to entertain legions of readers with fun books you enjoy writing, then writing to market is the way to go. I have many, many friends who've followed this model. They're still writing things they enjoy, but those things are also popular enough that they can earn a living. Below I'll present you with two examples of people who've adopted this model.

Cady Vance

I met Cady on the Writer's Cafe over at Kboards roughly a month after I started self-publishing. She's a Tennessee native transplanted to the U.K. where she just earned her doctorate in Creative Writing.

When Cady first self-published she was writing young adult novels. They were clever, fun, and *incredibly* well written. There was only one problem. No one was buying them. Cady was a great writer, but she was frustrated, with no idea how to proceed.

Fortunately, Cady and I met a group of writers who showed us the secrets revealed in this book. They convinced Cady to try writing something else. Cady had always wanted to try writing romance, so she studied her market and put out her first series. Within thirty days she'd made more money than she had the *entire year* before that. Her romance series has been immensely popular, because she's learned how to deliver what her readers want.

Domino Finn

Domino was in the same boat as Cady. I met him around the same time and he'd written an awesome book by the name of Seventh Sons. It's Sons of Anarchy, with frigging werewolves. I loved it. Unfortunately, it didn't conform to market tropes and sales numbers were disappointing. This despite how well written the book was.

Domino took a hard look at his work, then made a difficult decision. He finished up his series with a third book, and decided to write something entirely different. Domino's book *Dead Man* was written to appeal to Urban Fantasy fans who loved the Dresden Files. He knocked it out of the park and his books have been sticky in the top #5,000 since release. He's still writing books he enjoys, but now he's making a living doing it.

In Cady's case she switched to a whole different genre.

Domino stuck with the same genre, but approached it in a new way. In both cases, and this is critical, the authors in question were still writing what they love.

What do you love?

Now that you've seen a few examples showing this is possible, let's take a look at how the authors above did what they did, and how you can do the same.

It starts by picking something you enjoy writing. If you don't like what you write, then why would you pick this as a career? Most writers don't make a ton of money, and there are far easier ways to earn a living. Writing is very, very hard work. If you're going to crank out books, then you should crank out books that you love.

In my case that means science fiction, fantasy, horror, and non-fiction. I love that subject matter, so when I write to market those are the genres I'm looking at.

What do readers love?

I spent several hours browsing science fiction and fantasy books on Amazon. You'll learn how to do that effectively in the Analyzing the market section, but for now all you need to know is that there are categories and subcategories. An example category is Science Fiction. Subcategories include things like Space Operas, Colonization, Alien Contact, etc.

The top books in each of these categories are ranked by number of sales. Anything in the top #20 is on the first page a reader sees, and is usually there because readers found something that resonated in the book. I looked through these categories to see what those books were like. Were people more into Star Wars stories? Game of Thrones like stories? Dresden Files like stories?

A couple hours and a note pad gave me the answer. I checked overall rank on each book, which you can find about midway down the page. It will look something like this:

Amazon Best Sellers Rank: #4,535 Free in Kindle Store (See Top 100 Free in Kindle Store)

#6 in Kindle Store > Kindle eBooks > Mystery, Thriller & Suspense > Suspense > Paranormal > **Vampires**

#10 in Kindle Store > Kindle eBooks > Mystery, Thriller & Suspense > Suspense > Paranormal > **Werewolves & Shifters**

#10 in <u>Kindle Store</u> > <u>Kindle eBooks</u> > <u>Mystery, Thriller &</u> <u>Suspense</u> > <u>Suspense</u> > **Horror**

The lower the rank, the better. If the top book in a given category is in the top #1000 books on Amazon, then that is an extremely hot book. If the #20 book in that category is ALSO in the top #1000 you've found a red hot category that probably has an immense amount of competition. That means it will be extremely difficult for you to break into.

What you're looking for is a category where the #1 book is ranked really well, but the #20 book is only ranked moderately well. This generally indicates that the market is a good one, but isn't yet saturated with 8 billion clones of the top selling book.

If all this is clear as mud, don't worry. Later in the book I'll provide specific examples of what genre I did this with, and why I selected the one I selected.

Where is the intersection?

Once I knew what readers were buying I compared it to what I loved to write. Science fiction has always been a love of mine, and military science fiction is really hot right now. At least six books with giant starships on the cover are in the Amazon top #1000 right now. To get there those books are selling hundreds of copies a day. That tells me that there is a market for that kind of fiction.

The #20 book sits at an achievable rank of #2,000, while the #40 book is down at #8,000. This suggests that there are a lot of readers, but not enough books to satisfy them. Ding, ding, ding. We've found a winner.

Is the genre hungry?

Once I identified my genre it was time to begin the real research. That's the subject of the entire next 3 chapters, and we'll go in depth on what steps you need to take. What's the purpose of this in depth investigation? It isn't just to figure out the type of books people want to read. People love Harry Potter, but if you write a Harry Potter clone the only copies you sell will probably be to yourself and your mother.

Why? Because the child wizard trope has been done to death. If you go to the teen / fantasy category you'll find it littered with books about kids learning magic. If you peruse the top #200 books in that category you'll see countless series trying to hit the same mark. It's been done over and over, and unless you do it better, and get lucky, you're not going to have the success you're after.

What you need is a hungry genre that isn't yet saturated. That's a genre that loves to read, but isn't being supplied with enough books. A few years back that genre was Steampunk, as Lindsay Buroker proved. She wrote to market, and because the genre was small and sparsely populated, her books took off.

Right now military science fiction is underserved. There aren't enough great books about giant spaceships, so my next attempt at writing to market is aimed squarely at that genre. It's hungry, and I want to feed it.

A Quick Note About Exercises

Like my previous books every chapter in Write to Market ends with an exercise, and this book will be useless to you if you don't do them. However, you might be sitting on a bus right now in a position to keep reading, but not to do the first exercise. If you'd prefer to read the entire book before doing any exercises that's fine. You'll find the complete list in the Appendix at the back of the book. Just make sure you do them, or this book will have almost no value to you.

Exercise #1- Find your Market

Write down the top three genres you enjoy writing in. It doesn't matter what those genres are, as long as you find them fun and interesting. Now open up www.amazon.com and browse the top selling books in each of those categories. What commonalties do you see between them? Women wielding magic? Giant spaceships? Down on their luck P.I.s? Click on the #1 book, and the #20 book in each category, and jot down that book's rank.

Which of these areas do you think you'd most enjoy writing? Scroll through the top #100 books in your chosen genre. Ideally the books on the last two pages should have ranks higher than #25,000. If they do, then congratulations, you have found the right intersection.

Chapter 2- Tropes

What the hell is a trope, anyway? I first stumbled across the term over a decade ago when I discovered the site tvtropes.com. The technical definition of a trope is a figure of speech, but for our purposes it represents a plot trick, a narrative structure, a character type or any other recognizable storytelling device. A cliffhanger is a trope. So is the angry police chief who shouts at the protagonists in action movies.

Tropes are used in every form of story you're familiar with-- from books, to movies, to video games. If you want to write to market, you need to understand what they are, and how to employ them. Every genre has specific tropes. The rest of this chapter will provide examples, then a few guidelines on how you can pick out the tropes in the genre you chose in the last chapter.

Each one of the tropes below is something that readers will *recognize*. They've seen it before in some form, and while you can (and should) use it differently than other authors, your version must still be recognizable.

Major Tropes

These tropes, also called themes, are the overarching and easily recognizable ones. They usually refer to the largest plot or setting structures.

Minor Tropes

These tropes are smaller, but just as important. They usually apply to a single character, setting, or plot device. Both Major and Minor tropes are important to writing a successful novel, and interleaving them is an art form we all need to master.

Romance

Romance is a difficult genre for me to mine, as I don't know it very well. I turned to Rich Amooi and Cady Vance for help, and these are some of the tropes they taught me about.

Major Tropes

- HEA (happily ever after). This is the cornerstone of nearly all romance

HFN (happy for now). Some romance uses this, but it is more

niche.

Minor Tropes

Hero & Heroine meet

Hero & Heroine have a conflict

The story will reach a crisis point where our H&H look like they may not make it

There are many, many other tropes in Romance (and every other genre), but most of the ones I ran across were specific to a sub genre. For those interested, a quick Google search of Romance Tropes will give you a nearly inexhaustible supply.

Military Science Fiction

MSF is easier for me to mine for tropes, since it's the genre I'm currently writing. I researched the work of Joshua Dalzelle, Nick Webb, and Vaughn Heppner. Each of their books hit the top 1000, and all have similar themes. Most of those themes borrow heavily from shows like Star Trek and Battlestar Galactica.

Major Tropes

Humanity attacked by mysterious new enemy

Humanity attacked by long vanished enemy

Overbearing and incompetent military leadership

One ship and crew must save us all

Minor Tropes

Aging Starship aka Battlestar Galactica

Maverick Captain aka Kirk

Mystery

This one is easier than romance, but harder than military science fiction. I haven't read a lot of mystery, but I understand the formula most of the books take. For our purposes I'm describing Cozy Mysteries, which are a much tamer flavor than say Hard Boiled.

Major Tropes

Female amateur sleuth caught in mystery by accident

Hot sheriff or FBI agent who is investigating the case

Mystery solved in a happy ending (no cliffhangers, ever)

Almost no violence, and if it occurs it isn't described on

the page

Minor Tropes

Protagonist owns a yarn shop, cupcake business, etc

Victim is usually unpopular, and everyone had a reason to murder them

Wisecracking, match-making granny

Set in small town

Epic Fantasy

This one is also easy, as I've been a voracious reader since I was a kid. Epic fantasy is a broad genre, but one with surprisingly common tropes

Major

Ordinary boy finds out he is the Chosen One

The Dark One

Minor

Magical sword of awesome sauce

Kindly Mentor aka Gandalf

Animal sidekick

Snarky rival aka Draco Malfoy

There are countless tropes for countless genres, and you will never learn them all. That's totally okay. The ones you need to be familiar with are the most commonly used ones in your genre. If you can understand and nail those, you're 60% of the way to writing a marketable novel.

Handle Tropes With Care

Tropes are wonderful tools, but they can be very dangerous if misused. Have you ever seen a preview for a movie that had you as excited as a six year old on their birthday, but when you finally saw the movie it was a total let down? Nine times out of ten that let down was caused by misused tropes, and most often those misused tropes relate to characters.

Every story is ultimately about characters, and how they are affected by their adventure. From Woody in Toy Story to Frodo in Lord of the Rings we the audience are affected not by the plot, so much as how the characters react to it. The vital element separating mediocre stories from great ones is the characters. There's a reason people binge read 15+ Dresden books, and that reason is Harry Dresden and the supporting cast. The reason both TV viewers and readers have slogged through Game of Thrones is, once again, the strength of the characters within.

Your characters need to be likable, believable, and flawed. If you're writing Urban Fantasy, your hero or heroine should be snarky, but not an ass. If you're writing military science fiction your captain should be flawed, but ultimately do the right thing when under pressure. Every genre has its tropes, and the execution of those tropes is what will set you apart.

This is where craft matters. You need layered, nuanced characters that the readers in your chosen genre will love. The way those characters act should be different depending on genre. Katniss from the Hunger Games is a great example of a teenager reacting to very difficult circumstances. She is a very realistic portrayal of how a strong teen would handle the chaos thrown at her. That's exactly what the author intended, and why fans of that series love her so much. She's realistic and flawed. If I tried writing a Katniss like character in military science fiction people would drop the book by chapter two, because it doesn't matter how great the character is. It also has to fit the genre.

Think about Commander Adama from Battlestar Galactica. He's hard-edged, but caring. He does his duty, but compassion clouds his judgement when either his son Lee, or his surrogate daughter Starbuck are involved. He makes mistakes, but when the pressure is on he always rises to the occasion. That's why we the audience love him, and it's why a character like that works so well in military science fiction.

If you want to successfully write to market, you need the right tropes, and you need to employ them like a master. Write great characters that match your genre, and your readers will follow you for life.

Exercise #2- Pick your favorite book or movie, the one you've seen / read countless times. Write out a list of ten tropes. These should be tropes you've seen in other books and movies. For example, Star Wars employs tropes like Chosen One, and Kindly Mentor. What other ones can you identify?

Chapter 3- Which Books?

You've picked a genre, and you now have a general sense of what the tropes in that genre are. Now it's time to verify your hypothesis. To do that you need to find books that already have the kind of success you're after. This is trickier than it might sound, but this chapter will give you a concise overview of exactly how you do it.

In the next chapter we'll break down how books are successful, but before we get there we need to find the right ones. I'm going to use military science fiction / space opera for my examples here, as Star Wars Episode VII came out and just about everyone I know saw it. For those who aren't science fiction fans bear with me, and know that this formula applies to your genre as well.

What Not to Look for

If you go to the Space Opera section of Kindle books the first page displays the top 20 books. As of this writing #1 is

The Atlantis World, by A.G. Riddle. A quick peek at this book reveals that it isn't a space opera. It's #1, because it is listed in a whole bunch of categories, and is enormously popular overall. You'll see the same thing with George R.R. Martin's Game of Thrones being listed as science fiction. It clearly isn't, but many authors will list their book in multiple categories to reach more readers. That's generally a bad idea, as we'll discuss later.

Books 2 through 11 are all bad examples for us to emulate. Some for the same reason as The Atlantis World, they don't fit in our genre. The rest? They're bad to choose because they're published by the big 5 New York Publishers. You can usually tell this before clicking on the book, because they'll be priced much higher than the indie books that you want to mimic. Many are $9.99. How are they so highly ranked then? Because the publishers in question are pushing them. In a month or two most will fade to obscurity, but whether they do or don't the fact remains that we tiny authors cannot mimic their success.

You can ignore books like *The Force Awakens* and *Leviathan Wakes*. One is backed by the largest motion picture of all time, the other a top billed science fiction series on the SyFy channel. They're oranges, and we're apples.

Indie Published Books

We have to go all the way down to #12 to find what we're
looking for. That book is entitled *The Lost Starship*, and it is
absolutely perfect for our purposes. It's published by Vaughn
Heppner, an indie author, just like us. You can tell this by
searching Amazon for *The Lost Starship*. If you scroll down to
the Product Details section you'll find the publisher. It will
look like this:

Product Details

    File Size: 1739 KB

    Print Length: 438 pages

    Simultaneous Device Usage: Unlimited

    Publication Date: October 25, 2014

    Sold by: Amazon Digital Services LLC

If it's listed as Amazon Digital Services, that means it's
been self-published.

The Lost Starship has over 3,000 reviews, and is currently
ranked #585 in the store. That means it's selling over 100
copies a day, probably closer to 300. It was released in August

of 2014 (also visible under Product Details), which means it's been selling like hot cakes for almost two years. Wow. This is exactly the kind of success we all hope for with a book, so we have a winner.

Make Sure the Book is Sticky

Before selecting the first book you want to study check the price. Is it 99 cents? If so, there's a good chance the book is on sale. It may have just been featured in a major promotion, in a massive newsletter like BookBub, or some other media outlet. That could mean that this book is normally poorly ranked, and that in a week or two it might sink back there.

Check the number of reviews, and compare them against there publication date (you can see that under the Product Details displayed above). Ideally the book has 1,000 or more reviews, and hasn't been out for more than a year. If it's older than that it should have a lot more reviews, and if it has less than that it should be very recently released. For example, if a book came out two months ago and has 400 reviews that book is doing great. 400 reviews on a book that released in 2011 is much less impressive.

Why did the Book Succeed?

So how did Vaughn get his book so high up in the rankings? A quick peek at his website shows that this isn't his first series. He's put out several science fiction series, which means he probably has a good sized mailing list. That likely helped him launch this book, as it probably translated into a lot of early reviews and purchases. If you're a new author you don't have that advantage. So what do you do?

Find another book. I kept scanning down the list until I reached #19. There I found *Warrior*, book 2 of Nick Webb's Legacy Fleet trilogy. Book 1, Constitution, has nearly 1,300 reviews and only launched in June of 2015. It's hanging strong in the Amazon rankings at #1400 after 7 months. That's nothing short of amazing, and it's the kind of impact we want to have.

What makes this so important is that Nick has no other science fiction books. This is his first foray into Space Opera, so odds are good Nick didn't have a massive mailing list to work with. He launched this series cold, and it's blowing up. How did he do that?

Nick is hitting the right tropes. He has the right cover.

He has a great blurb. It's all the ingredients to get his target audience to purchase his book. In the next chapter we'll break down exactly what Nick did right.

Also Bought Books

I'd like to throw one last caveat your way before you find your own books. Once you've identified the right kind of book you can very quickly find others. Every Amazon product has a section under the description called Also Bought. This shows items that are most commonly bought by the person who bought what you're looking at.

In the case of *Constitution* (Nick's book), you'll see a whole bunch of other books with giant spaceships on the cover. Most of these books belong to Joshua Dalzelle, Vaughn Heppner, or B.V. Larson. That isn't a coincidence. I'll bet you a nickel that Nick studied the genre carefully before writing, and *Constitution* is similar to those other authors' work because he realized their work was hitting exactly the right tropes.

Because he did his work well, his book shows up in *their* also bought items, which is part of why his book sells so well. That kind of organic discovery is invaluable, and if you do your work well it's exactly what your book should have.

Exercise #3- Pick Books to Emulate

Go to Amazon and examine the top #20 books in your genre. Which ones are indie published? What is their ranking? How many reviews do they have? How long have they been out? Most importantly, how many books did the author publish in that genre before the book you're looking at took off?

Repeat this process until you have three books to use as case studies. We'll examine those books in depth in the next section.

Bonus: Spend time perusing the Also Bought books for each of the books you select. What commonalities do you see between covers and titles?

Chapter 4- Analyzing Your Market

We've now seen that it's very possible for an indie author to break into a new genre, kicking the crap out of the Amazon charts in the process. It's possible to do this without being the next Andy Weir or Hugh Howey. You don't need to be a break out box office hit to make a six figure living selling books. Nick Webb, Vaughn Heppner, and B.V. Larson have all done it with science fiction.

Rosalind James and Annie Jacoby have done it in romance. Libbie Hawker has done it in historical fiction. Lindsay Buroker has done it in steampunk. I'm doing it with non-fiction, sci-fi thrillers, and as of the time of this writing am about to (hopefully) do it again with military science fiction.

Let's see how others are doing it, so you can do it too.

You're going to have to *gasp* read

One of the things that surprised me a great deal when I started networking with other authors is that almost none of them read. I very quickly made an interesting correlation. The authors who DID read were the successful ones. The ones who didn't were generally floundering, unable to achieve the level of success they were after.

If you want to succeed as an author you need to work your ass off. Not only do you need to work, but you need to work intelligently. That means reading a LOT. You need to read in every genre, and you most especially need to read the genre you want to write.

Before you can truly understand why books are successful, you have to read the frigging books. You can't just look at the blurb and cover to understand why that book took off. The author's voice, their subject matter, pacing, and tropes are all critical to their book's success. Want to mimic it? Then read their work and study how they did all of those things.

When I decided to write my military science fiction series I went for total immersion. I began re-watching Battlestar Galactica, because I realized the books I selected in the last chapter all borrowed heavily from that show. I started re-playing the Mass Effect video game series, because a few of them borrowed from that too.

Then I started reading *Constitution*. I moved on to *Warship*. Right now I'm reading *The Lost Starship*. I will continue to read and analyze successful military science fiction until I've written and published my own. Not only does reading these books show me what the other authors did right, it also ensures that I'm not accidentally copying their plots. I can write something I think readers will like, without re-hashing their books.

There's also one other huge benefit. I love science fiction, so I get to read books I love. If I didn't love them, then I probably shouldn't be writing in this genre anyway.

What Tropes are Being Used?

A long vanished enemy returns. Mankind has grown complacent. Their newest military technology is no match for their enemy. Their only hope is an aging starship that was about to be decommissioned and set up as a floating museum. A dying leader. An alcoholic XO. What am I describing? If you said Battlestar Galactica, you're right. If you said Nick Webb's *Constitution* you'd also be right.

Nick utilized the same tropes as one of the most beloved science fiction shows ever. He's taken some flak in reviews (we'll discuss mining reviews for expectations later), but the vast majority of his readers loved his book. Why? Because it was familiar. They'd seen each of the pieces before, but never assembled in quite this way. Nick had an interesting new enemy, the swarm. He had all new characters, even though we'd seen some of the specific tropes before. He had short punchy chapters, tight pacing, and a great ending.

War is a thing of the past. Humanity has explored the stars for five centuries without meeting an alien race. Their machines of war are ancient and decrepit. A new enemy suddenly appears, and starts kicking mankind's ass. Against incredible odds one captain with an aging warship must triumph over an implacable foe.

Warship, the title of this book, is a little less recognizable, but also borrows from Star Trek and BSG. Notice some of the similarities to *Constitution*. Aging Starship. Maverick Captain. A seemingly unstoppable enemy. Military leadership that gets in the way.

Humanity is woefully outclassed. One maverick captain and his misfit crew will have to stop the New Men. To do that he needs a ship that was left behind thousands of years ago by a long vanished alien culture. This is from the book *The Lost Starship*.

Are you spotting some trends? I know I did, and here they are:

Major Tropes

- Every book has a maverick captain, and a misfit crew.

- The captain succeeds in spite of an inept government

- The captain and his aging warship are totally outclassed by their opponents

- Mankind's survival looks dubious

- Every cover has a gigantic, badass spaceship on it

Minor Tropes

- All three books have their own version of faster than light travel

- All three books use military lingo. CAG, CIC, etc

- Two of the three books have a junior officer at odds with the captain. That junior officer has been assigned by military command.

- There is a cost to victory. Someone is going to die, and / or large swathes of the human fleet are going to get wiped out

Each plot is notably different, but they all hit those

specific tropes. I read all three books, and each was different enough that reading the others didn't detract from my enjoyment. That's because all three authors are doing their job well. They wrote an original plot, with familiar tropes. Readers want to know that the big pieces they love are present, but they also want those pieces to be used in new and interesting ways.

The enemies in all three books are different. The solutions to defeat the enemies are different. The captains and crews are different. But they are similar enough to feel familiar, and thus resonate with readers. More on that in the We Have To Go Deeper chapter.

More on the Physical Similarities

The books listed above have several similarities that extend beyond tropes. They are all roughly the same length, between 60-70k words. They all have similar cover artwork, enough that the reader can easily identify the genre. All three blurbs mention the same tropes. Even their prices are the same, between $3.99 and $5.99, with the $5.99 belonging to the author with the greatest following, and $3.99 belonging to the author with the least.

The parallels I've used for the military science fiction example absolutely hold true for other genres. You'll see similar trends in romance, epic fantasy, westerns, steampunk, and any other genre you're interested in writing. Knowing what those conventions are is vital if you want to be successful. If you try writing a 30k epic fantasy it will crash and burn. Fantasy readers like long books. Likewise, if you write a 300k word erotica novel you're going to have difficulty selling it.

Exercise #4- This one is a doozy. Pick one of the books you researched in the last chapter. Read it, and as you're reading jot down notes on the tropes you see used. What's working in the book? What isn't? What makes this book similar to others in the genre, and how could you use the same tropes in new ways?

Bonus: Repeat this process for two more books.

Chapter 5- We Have to Go Deeper

Ideally you've completed the exercise in the last chapter, but since many of you want to finish this entire book before doing the exercises I know that's unlikely. It's totally okay if you haven't, but you may want to revisit this chapter (and the rest of the book) once you've read at least one of the top selling books in your genre.

If I had to recommend one skill outside of craft that every writer needs to study it would be psychology. I cannot overstate the importance of understanding how the human mind works. If you want to tell great stories, you need to know why people consider them great. Myth and story have existed since humans huddled around fires in caves. They've been a counterpoint to human development, and if you understand how and why they are important to the human psyche you will go far as a writer.

It isn't enough to know what tropes to use, to assemble them like so many legos. If that's all you study, then you'll just end up churning out another Hunger Games clone. If you want to make it as an author you need to understand *why* readers react to specific tropes.

Why Readers Read

Every reader picks up a book for different reasons, but all of us are transported to another time and place when we do. The question you need to ask when considering what to write is *why do the people I want to write for pick up books*?

Most authors never ask this question, yet some of them turn out incredibly addictive books. This generally happens because they're writing books they themselves want to read. That appeals to other readers who want to read the same type of books, which is why some authors easily find an audience.

I experienced this first hand when I wrote *No Such Thing As Werewolves*. I combined the following:

1- I was annoyed that werewolves and vampires were no longer scary

2- I loved the idea that there might be a long vanished culture mankind has forgotten all about

3- I liked the idea of suddenly gaining super powers

4- I find the idea that the sun could, at any time, destroy all our technology utterly terrifying

5- I often wonder how I'd handle a zombie apocalypse

I didn't realize it when I was writing the book, but I was penning a classic thriller. There was a pair of intertwining mysteries that had to be solved before the clock counted down to 0. I raised the stakes in every chapter, and had larger than life confrontations. I had ordinary characters placed in extraordinary situations, who rose to the occasion no matter what it cost.

People loved it, and the book still sells far more copies than I'd ever dreamed it could. When I began my next series I started asking myself why. Why did readers love it? Why did they identify with my characters, and what did they get out of the things I'd written? What did I get out of them?

The answers were interesting, and they began with looking at my own motivations. I wanted to believe that there was still wonder in the world. We've explored the globe. We've mapped the oceans. We've been to the moon, and Mars. Our solar system is explored. We know a great deal about human evolution, and about where we as a species came from.

It isn't until we get back to nine or ten thousand years ago that we start having real questions. The idea that there could be something we haven't discovered yet really resonates with me, because I hate thinking that all the big discoveries have already happened. In essence, I want a new frontier. *No Such Thing As Werewolves* delivered that new frontier. It gave the sense of wonder I so desperately craved, the same sense of wonder that people who loved the book were after.

I did this in two ways, each a hallmark of a different genre. The first genre was urban fantasy. People have long enjoyed stories of vampires and werewolves. Most current fiction has these supernatural critters hiding in plain sight. They have elaborate societies lurking just outside human perception, and often the main character's journey involves them learning of this secret world.

The second way was far more at home in science fiction. The idea that an ancient culture exists, one far more advanced than ours, isn't new. I took that idea and ran with it, offering something that surpasses any legends of Atlantis.

Lastly, I tossed in a world ending apocalypse. At any moment the sun could discharge a coronal mass ejection, which would wipe out electronics all over the globe. We've seen smaller bursts twice in history, and I referenced both in the novel. That resonated with people, because while they are afraid of the changes something like that could cause, they also crave a fresh start. Our world is polluted. It's overcrowded. It's corrupt. What if someone or something pressed the reset button? How would we react?

Post-apocalyptic stories allow readers to answer those questions from the relative comfort of their living room. That's powerful stuff, and I tapped into it without even understanding that's what I was doing.

That's great, but how does one go about that sort of analysis with a much more conscious approach?

Mining Reviews for Reader Expectations

The first place I look for information on reader psychology is in the reviews. This is especially easy if the book has a large number of them. You aren't looking for the three star reviews. You want either five star or one star, because both provoked the most extreme reaction. These will be the people who either loved or hated the book, and you can easily puzzle out why by examining a half dozen of each.

These reviews must be specific. Quite a few will be short, vague, and useless. It's the ones who explain why they liked or hated something that will be useful. Read as many of those as you can, and you'll start to pick up trends.

For *No Such Thing As Werewolves* the negative reviews all highlight the same thing. I had inaccuracies. Some of my information about firearms was wrong. I mistakenly said Saturn when I meant Neptune. The helicopter I chose wasn't used in the Vietnam War. That taught me a valuable lesson. Readers of thrillers, especially thrillers with even a twinge of military action, crave accuracy at the expense of all else.

The positive reviews also followed a similar theme. The coherent ones talked about how I pulled together a series of seemingly unrelated events into a tightly woven plot. By the end of the book they were left muttering 'holy shit', because I'd made the idea that werewolves, ancient pyramids, power armor, a solar apocalypse, AIDS, and zombies were all somehow related.

In both cases I learned about reader expectations. If you hit them, readers will devour your work. If you miss them, they'll trash you publicly, and they won't buy anything else from you. Ever.

Helpful Reviews

Every review on Amazon, iTunes, or Audible allows a user to flag it as either helpful or unhelpful. This is very important to our research. If you see a one star review with 1 out of 24 helpful votes, then the vast majority of readers disagreed with it. You should give it less weight. If you see a review with 44 out of 48 helpful votes, that means it resonated with a lot of readers. This is how both five star and one star reviews get to the first page on places like Amazon.

The one star reviews for Constitution that compare it to Battlestar Galactica have a lot of up votes. A significant number of readers resonate with them. Not all, as evidenced by the massive number of positive reviews. But enough that we should pay attention. If those reviews were not on the front page, and had less helpful votes, I'd have paid a lot less attention to them.

Studying Readers

I recommend taking a good chunk of time to study your readers, and this is easier than you might expect. Once I'd read a few well written 5 star reviews, and a few well written one star reviews, I clicked on each of those reviewer's profiles. You can see what else they've rated, which teaches you a lot about what type of person you're dealing with. Some of those reviewers one star everything. Some have never reviewed another book.

Most, however, have reviewed quite a few books. They've usually given a range of reviews. By finding what they give a five star to, and what they one star, you can learn what their expectations are. When they purchased *No Such Thing As Werewolves, Constitution*, or any other book, they did so because they had certain expectations. They wanted a certain type of story, and the blurbs, titles, and covers used made them think they were going to get that type of story.

If they gave it 5 stars, then you met or exceeded those expectations. If you got a one star, you missed the mark. That doesn't mean that you did anything wrong. Every book will get one stars, from *The Lord of the Rings* to *The Martian*. The important thing is learning who will give your book a one star, and who will absolutely love it.

If you spend a little time studying some of the top reviewers for the books you'll learn about both types of readers, which will help you figure out what kind of story you need to write.

5,000 Words Per Hour

Around the time I learned about reader expectations I wrote
5,000 Words Per Hour. Identifying reader expectations was easy
for non-fiction, especially because I was writing toward a
demographic that I was a part of. Writers. I simply looked at
myself and identified the single biggest constraint, the thing
that was preventing me from achieving the success I was after.

Every writer I know wants to write faster. I've read every
book on the subject that I can get my hands on. That motivation
is very, very easy to understand, and since you're reading this
I suspect it's one you share.

Once I understood the problem it was easy to write a book
that would hit all the right notes. I identified the problem,
and crafted the best book I could to solve it. That solution has
been widely embraced, and I've sold a ton of copies as a result.
It's the same principle you utilize when writing fiction.

I also have my fair share of one star reviews. Some call me
a liar. Others say writing quickly will never work. There's a
common thread to all of them, though. They believe that writing
fast equals writing crap, and nothing I say or do will change
their mind. They are a small, and not terribly vocal minority.

My Next Experiment

In the previous few chapters we've stuck with military science fiction, so I'll continue that here. Let's jump back to the first book we examined, Nick Webb's *Constitution*. I loved this book, and so did most of the 1,300 people who reviewed it. You'd never know that from reading the first page of reviews though. Almost all the ones on the first page are one star, and boy do they trash the book.

The pattern we see in those reviews is very straightforward. They feel it hews too closely to the show Battlestar Galactica, and they feel cheated as a result. They're annoyed, because instead of enjoying a fresh new story, they feel like they're reading something they've already experienced.

If you look at the reviews for *The Lost Starship* every review on the first page is a one star. People say the writing sucks. They point out that the captain is basically Kirk (though no one uses that comparison). They say the book could have been written for teenagers, and is very simplistic. Those people are a small, but very vocal minority.

This information is very, very useful, because it tells us who won't like the book, and more importantly *why* they won't like the book.

What do we do with this information?

The negative reviews discussed in the last section tell us something vital. They identify exactly the type of reader who *hated* the book. When you combine that with the information you can glean from the five star reviews you come up with a very interesting picture.

I'd initially assumed that most space opera / military science fiction readers would be veterans from the marines, army, or navy. I couldn't have been more wrong. Readers who were in a branch of the service were the ones dropping the one star reviews. The ones giving 5 star reviews were the people who *wished* they'd been in the service. They didn't know enough about military procedure, discipline, fraternization or physics to care about inaccuracies.

Readers who enjoyed *The Lost Starship*, *Warship*, and *Constitution* don't care about Faulkner level prose, or that the plots aren't incredibly complex. They enjoy that the captains are an uncomplicated throwback to 60s Star Trek. I started thinking about why, since I fall into that demographic. The reason was astoundingly simple. Most of us see a dark, grim world around us. A world where we aren't able to affect any sort of meaningful change.

When we read a science fiction novel not only do we get to see a wondrous new world, but we also get to make a difference. We save the galaxy from a catastrophic threat, instead of whatever mind numbingly boring day job we might do. In short, we're reading these novels to escape from our dreary lives into fantastic worlds.

How does that information influence the story I'm going to write? Here are a list of observations:

- Mankind is being attacked, and only our maverick captain and his plucky crew can stop the scary new enemy

- Their warship is outdated and held together with duct tape and string

- Fleet command will get in the way

- I don't need to worry so much about the specifics of guns, ships, and raw science. Getting those details right is good, but *most* readers will forgive occasional lapses

- I need a happy ending. The protagonist has to succeed, even if there is a cost in doing so. This means that the story must be self-contained. A series is fine, but there must be a hard ending in each book. Cliffhangers will piss people off.

- Showing a race of aliens, or even two, is just fine. Trying to present dozens of them like Star Wars does will overly complicate things, and alienate readers. Think Star Trek. You've got the occasional Klingon or Vulcan, but the vast majority of the cast is human.

- Game of Thrones style character deaths will not play well. My target readers aren't looking for Grimdark. Offing a side character here or there might work, but people don't want the cost of success to be too high.

You'll notice that none of these observations mean I have to write the same story as the books I showcased. I'm free to write an original tale, as long as I'm mindful of my readers. They prefer something that feels familiar, but that also breaks a little new ground. If you can do that, your fans will devour your work.

Exercise #5- This is another tough one, because this is the longest chapter in the book. Pick one of the books from your list. Read the top 5 negative reviews, and the top 5 positive. What trends are you spotting? What did more than one reader like or dislike? Why do you think that is? Do these reviews give you some idea of who your target reader should be? If you're unsure, then take a look at a few of the reader profiles. What books did they like / dislike? For the one star reviews why do you feel their expectations weren't met? Why were they met for the 5 star reviews?

Bonus: Repeat this process for each of the three books you selected. I know that this is time consuming, but this is one of the most critical exercises in the book. Investing time here will be immensely useful later.

Chapter 6- Don't Get Cute

Up until now you've heard mostly about my successes, and the successes of other authors. I've made this writing to market thing seem easy and intuitive, like I arrived at it on my first day as an author. That was, sadly, not the case. My first novel was accidentally written to market. I got lucky.

More recently I launched a spin off series called Project Solaris. The first book was called *Hero Born*, and as I mentioned earlier it is a cross between Heroes and X-Files. I was almost giddy with excitement, because Heroes (one of my all time favorite shows, the first season at least) was returning to the air. To my shock I learned that X-Files was too, and that IS my all time favorite show.

I was already mentally cashing the checks. Here I was writing a series that capitalized on both genres. Surely readers would love it, and I'd sell eight bazillion copies! Yeah, no. The book crashed and burned. My loyal Deathless readers eagerly gobbled it up, but almost no new readers took a chance on it. As of this writing it's sitting at #60,000 in the store, which is abysmal for a book that's only been out for five weeks.

Heroes Reborn was cancelled, and that X-Files reboot? It's two episodes in and fans are not impressed.

What Went Wrong

Conventional wisdom among indie authors suggests that I gave up on Hero Born too early. I knew within two weeks of launching that it had failed. My author buddies told me not to give up. They said I should play with the blurb, or consider a new cover, or maybe do a massive promotion. I did none of those things, outside of a promo I'd already scheduled. I knew precisely why Hero Born wasn't getting traction, and nothing I did was going to change that. The flaw was in the writing, not the packaging.

Why did Hero Born fail so spectacularly? Because *I didn't meet reader expectations*. Repeat that out loud, because it's that important. Is *Hero Born* a good book? People who've read it say yes, but only a few hundred have. Contrast that to the tens of thousands who read (and continue to read) my Deathless series.

Here's the crux of the issue. Superheroes is a hot genre. Alien conspiracies and invasions are also a hot genre. Mixing them alienated readers of both. Cheeseburgers are great, and so is ice cream, but try mixing them and you'll be hard pressed to find someone who wants to eat lunch with you.

Superhero novels rely on a young protagonist just discovering their powers. Books like Logan Rutherford's *The Second Super*, and Tom Reynolds *Meta* hit the same tropes. Their biggest demographic seems to be teens, which makes sense given the subject matter. The antagonist is, unsurprisingly, a *super villain*.

Alien conspiracy books aren't as popular right now, but the ones that are selling feature average joe protagonists discovering the alien threat. Think Zane from the movie The Arrival, or Fox Mulder from the X-Files.

Remember when we figured out why readers enjoy military science fiction? Let's use the same logic here, at a higher level. Why do people enjoy superhero books? My unscientific guess is that readers want to feel special. The protagonist in superhero novels generally starts out normal, but gains super human abilities that set them apart. I know that would have appealed to me in high school. Hell it appeals to me today.

How about readers of Alien Conspiracy style books? They're uncovering a deeper truth, one the government is keeping hidden. Those books are more about mystery, and about the restoration of natural order when the protagonist reveals the threat to the world at large.

There isn't a lot of overlap between the two types of readers, and it's unlikely that readers of one genre will cross to the other. That is why *Hero Born* failed, and why it will likely remain a niche book only purchased by fans of my other books.

My protagonist is a 21 year old intern for a San Francisco startup, making him too old for fans of super hero books. The villain(s) are aliens, not a traditional super villain. Right there you can see I've lost the entire superhero crowd. The protagonist fights back against the aliens, manifesting cool super powers, and gradually uncovering their evil plot. That's unfamiliar to readers of Alien Conspiracy, so I've lost a few of them too.

Mistakes Rock

Am I upset that I wrote *Hero Born*? Heck no. I had a blast writing it, and the fans who have read it, love it. The problem is that books like *Hero Born* aren't going to pay my rent. If I want to do that, I need to write to market. That more than anything else is why I wrote this book, because I'm learning from my mistake.

In later chapters we'll talk about speed of execution, learning from failed launches, and measuring success. You'll begin to see why *Hero Born* was very valuable. It taught me a lot about reader expectations, as will every book I ever release from here forward. Some of those books will fail like *Hero Born* did, but the important distinction is that I will know why they failed. That makes it possible to succeed, because future books will benefit from that knowledge.

It's totally fine to miss the mark, as long as you learn from it.

Hit Expectations

A final note about hitting expectations. When I plotted out my military science fiction book, Destroyer, I was very cognizant of reader expectations. I've done my homework carefully. One of the decisions I made was very difficult, but ultimately the right one. You may find it controversial.

I love strong female characters. My Deathless series is full of them, and my female werewolves are both larger and stronger than the males. That was both fun to write, and really resonated with readers of both genders.

My initial inclination in Destroyer was to make the captain a woman, but after launching my study of the genre I decided against it. Why? Because exactly zero of the top selling books had a female captain. Every last one had a male, aging, maverick captain. That's one of the cardinal tropes, and as much as it pains me, I've decided to adhere to it.

Here's the upside, though. I can't write a book without strong female characters. I just can't do it. So I added three, just in different roles. My pilot, my point of view marine, and an enemy captain are all female. That allows me to write the book I want to write, but adheres to the tropes I'll have to hit if I want to sell books.

Exercise #6 - This was the hardest exercise in the book for me. If you've already completed and / or published a novel I want you to take a hard look at it now. Did it sell the way you wanted it to? If it did not, then ask yourself why? Did you violate reader expectations, and if so how? What genre were you aiming for, and how does your book differ from the books in that genre?

Write out a bulleted list with the answers.

Chapter 7- Speed of Execution

Those of you who've read *5,000 Words Per Hour* will find no surprises here. One of the single most important parts of writing to market is speed of execution. Market tropes change very, very quickly. This year it could be military science fiction, but next year that might change to time travel mysteries. The longer you take to get your books to market, the more you risk launching after your target genre has peaked.

Some genres are more forgiving than others, but the unforgiving ones are merciless. If you write romance, for example, you'd better be pounding away on that keyboard as quickly as possible. Stepbrother Billionaire is king, until it isn't. Fantasy, on the other hand, is far more timeless and you have a little more wiggle room. Either way, though, speed of execution is vital.

Yes, But...

Writing a novel is difficult. The fewer books you've

written, the more daunting the prospect is. That is ten times as true if you're writing your first novel. It took me over two years the first time around, and that doesn't count the decade I spent filling up my hard drive with half finished books.

So what if you're not a fast writer? Then you should strongly consider becoming one. It will take time and work, but let's be honest. If you want to succeed at this writing thing it's going to take you an ass ton of effort (that's an official measurement in Australia). If you're not the world's fastest typist, and you aren't cranking 5,000 words or more out each day that's okay.

Pick up a book on writing faster, like *5,000 Words Per Hour*, or *2k to 10k*. Start practicing writing sprints. Work every day to write just a little more, and to be consistent in your writing habit. If that latter part is difficult, hey I've got a book for that too. Check out *Lifelong Writing Habit*.

Whether you read the other books or no, you need to make production a big part of your writing. That means finishing what you start, and doing it as quickly as you realistically can without sacrificing quality.

Long Haul

Hopefully, you're in this for the long haul. You're willing to invest years, because that's what it's going to take to get to the top of this game. You aren't going to arrive there tomorrow, and you aren't going to arrive at all unless you want this badly enough to put in a great deal of work.

If you're currently turning out a novel a year, then can you do two this year? If you did two, can you do four? Push yourself, and you'll be surprised. Amanda Lee is writing 29 novels in 2016. I'm putting out 12 books. How many can you do? Is it more than last year?

Don't Be So Hard On Yourself

If you're not a writing powerhouse and it takes you two years to finish a book that's okay too. You can only write as fast as you can write, and as long as you're working as hard as you can that's what matters. The trick is not to give up. You need to keep writing, and you need to focus on the small wins. If you can finish your next book a little faster than the last, that's a win. If you sell a handful more copies than the last book, that's a win.

This game is all about incremental improvement, and that means it's okay not to be king of the world just yet. As long as you keep writing, you will keep improving. So keep writing, and keep learning.

Iteration is Key

Hero Born was, as you read in the last chapter, a big failure in my book. How did I respond to that? I got back on the horse and wrote another book. You're holding it. Then I wrote another book, which may have already launched by the time you read this.

I don't get hung up on the success of any specific book. I learn what I can from launching it, then I use that experience to launch the next one. You need to do the same thing. Failure is okay. Stagnation is not. It doesn't matter how many books you've written, or how poorly they've done. What matters is how well the next one does, and once it's finished, how well the one after that does.

In the words of the immortal Johnny Truant and Sean Platt you must *Write, Publish, Repeat.*

Goal Setting

Only you know what a realistic time frame is to finish your next book. As stated above it doesn't matter so much what that time frame is, but what DOES matter is that you have a deadline. Deadlines are powerful, powerful stuff. They affect our subconscious in ways science is still figuring out, but the gist of it is this. You are almost a hundred times more likely to complete a goal if you:

1- Write that goal down

2- Set a specific date for its attainment

Exercise #7 - It's time to set your goals. Take a hard look at how long it took to write your last novel. Use that time frame to extrapolate how long it will take to write the next one. Can you do it a little faster? Pick a date. Write that date down on a sticky note and put it on your monitor with the title of the book you want to finish.

Also add that date to your calendar, and add a reminder one month from now that you're going to have the book done by then.

Bonus: Tell at least one friend about your goal.

Accountability helps far, far more than people assume.

Chapter 8- 80% is good enough

This chapter was both one of the hardest to write, and the hardest to accept as fact. It was drilled into my head by a good friend, the mysterious Mr. Market. I say mysterious because as the name suggests, I have no idea who he really is. I know him only through forum posts and emails, which have taught me an immense amount about this business. Mr. Market is a true master of writing to market, more so than anyone else I've ever met.

So what did he teach me that was so difficult to accept? 80% is good enough.

When I published *No Such Thing As Werewolves* I was mortified to learn there was a typo on the first page. It was the first of dozens, which were littered throughout my 130,000 word manuscript. I'd employed a line editor, and a separate proofreader. Yet tons of mistakes were missed anyway. I'd spent over $3,000 on editing, to what felt like no avail.

Worse, there were inaccuracies. I'd worked with several people I trusted when setting up firearms, military equipment, and some of the science. 95% of their information was accurate, but I still got some information wrong about firearms, used the wrong planet (Neptune instead of Saturn), and had a half dozen other embarrassing problems. None of my editors caught them, and neither did I.

I refined my process for the sequel, *No Mere Zombie*. This go around I used three editors, and I asked several beta readers to proofread as well. Even more typos slipped through. The editing was even worse than *No Such Thing As Werewolves*, despite me shelling out over $8,000 for editing in 2015.

By the time I out the third book in the series, *Vampires Don't Sparkle*, I'd learned a lot more about the process. I spent more of my own time editing, and weeded out most of the problems myself. It cost time, but in my mind it was worth that time. *Vampires Don't Sparkle* was my cleanest novel to date, because of that extra time and attention. I was incredibly proud of that fact.

Then Mr. Market slapped me upside the head with reality. Do you know how many people mentioned poor editing in *No Such Thing As Werewolves* reviews? Not a single one. I have over 800 across multiple stores, and not a single person mentioned typos. Exactly six people mentioned the inaccuracies I was so horrified by.

When I considered the ratio, I realized that a staggering 99.7% of reviewers didn't give two shits about a few typos or inaccuracies. Mr. Market asked me if it was worth all the time and money I spent editing. It slowed my production, and the sad reality was that better editing wasn't helping sales. So why was I doing it?

80 / 20 Publishing

For those not familiar with the Pareto principle the idea is that 80% of your success comes from 20% of your actions. This has been so true in so many areas, that it's now considered all but universal. From economics to publishing, Pareto is king. If you take a look at any part of your own life you'll find it's true.

How much of your success as a writer comes from writing every day? That's a 20% activity, because it produces 80% of your success. How about browsing forums like Kboards? How much do you get from that compared to writing every day? Social media is an 80% activity. It isn't your bread and butter. It's the fluff that you could cut out without noticeably impacting your level of success.

When Mr. Market forced me to examine my own publishing I realized he was right. I was spending a LOT of time and money getting my books edited. At first that editing was more valuable, because I wasn't as skilled at writing. Having a writing coach and a developmental editor helped me improve. But now that I'm on my 9th book? I don't need them as much, and am wasting both time and money trying to make my books a tiny bit better.

If you want to succeed at this game you need to be ruthless when examining which 20% of your actions are responsible for your success. Do you really need to do what you're doing? Could you offload that task to a virtual assistant? What would happen if you didn't overhaul your website?

It might not be immediately clear why I included this in a book about writing to market, but hear me out. If Mr. Market is right, and he has the publishing income to prove that he is, then you can get away with an imperfect book. Most of your readers will love it. Those who don't may give you a few bad reviews, but so what? Take a look back to some of the books we examined. *Constitution* and *The Lost Starship* both have one stars, some on the front page. But they have hundreds more five stars. *Most* readers love those books.

How much would those authors have gained if they'd spent another three or four months polishing their books? What if they'd eradicated a few more typos, or corrected the occasional inaccuracy? Would the 95% of readers who enjoyed their books have enjoyed them more? Probably not. It might have mollified a few of the people who left a one star, but odds are good many of them still would have. I don't care how good you are, you will get bad reviews.

So, knowing that, how much time should you spend polishing your book? Can you get away with less than you think you need? I'm about to find out.

Brutal Self-Assessment

I realize the previous section might sound a bit like 'Chris Fox says it's okay to pump out crap'. That's absolutely NOT what I'm saying. In the words of Robert Chazz Chute, you should strive for excellence, not perfection. You need a great story. You need tight pacing. You need good prose. Believable characters. Nor should you put out a book without proofreading. If this is your first book you should consider a writing coach, or a developmental editor. You should listen to what they say, and learn everything you can about being a better writer.

Your readers will ultimately decide if you're worth their

hard earned dollars and precious time, and if you cut corners before you've built the requisite skill you'll earn neither. Your goal should be continuous improvement. You want to be a better writer with each new book, and to have a more efficient process for getting it to market.

I used a writing coach for my second, third, and fourth novels. I learned a lot in the process, and I don't regret spending that time and money. It was an investment in myself. But now it's time to take it to the next level. Going forward I'll see what I can do without the support of a developmental editor, and instead I'll use the best feedback an author can have. Readers. They'll tell me if I'm good enough on my own, or if perhaps I need to go back to a more robust editing process.

If you're not already familiar with Heinlein's rules they absolutely apply here, particularly rule #3.

1- You Must Write

2- Finish What You Start

3- **Refrain from Rewriting, Except to Editorial Order**

4- You Must Put Your Story On the Market

5- You Must Keep It On The Market Until It has Sold

6- You Must Work on Something Else

Heinlein published 32 novels, 59 short stories, and 16 collections. Asimov published over 500 works. Do you think either of them wrote six drafts for every book? I seriously doubt it, and I don't think we should either. It's fine to write several drafts for your first book or two, because you're still learning the fundamentals. But you should always be looking for ways to improve both the quality of your writing, and your overall process.

Don't push out crap, just to get books out. But don't polish the same book for years on end.

Pen Names

My Project Solaris and Deathless series both have professional level editing. I've paid through the nose for it, and it remains unclear how much it's helped. So my next book, the military sci-fi you hear referenced throughout Write to Market, will only have a line editor. She'll look for typos, and I'll pay her for a single pass. Instead of using three editors that cost me several thousand dollars, I'll use one and keep costs around $500. Mr. Market argues I don't even need to do that much.

This caused a knee jerk reaction, of course. How could I release a novel without editing? What would my existing fans think? Mr. Market had an answer for that. Use a pen name. He has used many, creating and shedding them as he learns, and as marketing trends change.

It's possible my sci-fi series will bomb, and that readers will crucify me for poor editing. If the book fails, I can choose to jettison that pen name. If, and I think this is far more likely, the pen name does really well, then I can tell my existing fan base about it. But putting it under a pen name allows me to both segregate the genres I write, and insulate my main fan base from my brazen experiment.

I realize that you may find this process uncomfortable, and pen names are not for everyone. If you're not comfortable using them, and if you believe strongly that editing is critical, then please feel free to ignore that advice. At the end of the day you need to be proud of your work. Cutting corners is fine, but if you feel there's too much loss in quality, then trust your gut. Publishing is a business, sure, but if you feel that pen names don't fit your brand, then do what you feel is right.

Exercise #8 - Get out a pad of paper, or open a blank document in your word processor of choice. Write down each distinct part of your writing business. Everything from writing, to plotting, to reading books on craft, to updating your website, to chatting with other authors. Rate each of these activities from 1 to 10, with 10 contributing the most to your success as an author. This should make it immediately clear what's important, and what's not.

How much faster could you write if you cut out everything 6 or below, and outsourced your 7 and 8s to a virtual assistant? What if you focused 100% of your time on the 9s and 10s? What would your author business look like?

Bonus: Brainstorm a pen name for the first novel you write to market.

Chapter 9- Branding With a Red Hot Iron

There is only one major piece of writing to market remaining, and the only writing involved is copywriting. That last piece is branding. As we've mentioned throughout this book you need to create a novel that is both familiar, and unique. I say create instead of write, because part of that process has to do with packaging. If you follow the recipe this book provides your book could still fail spectacularly unless you focus on that last pivotal piece.

People are inherently visual creatures, and thanks to the never ending bombardment of advertising we've all been subjected to our attention spans shrink every year. That's made worse by having access to our smartphones during every waking moment. That means it is harder than ever to catch someone's attention. You're competing with every other author in your genre, with video games, movies, television and every other form of entertainment.

If you want people to read your book over all those other distractions, then you need to get them excited the very instant they encounter your book. There are four parts to that magical recipe, each described below.

Cover

Cover is, in my opinion, the single most important aspect of your book. This is doubly true of the thumbnail view, which is the first thing a reader will see. Imagine yourself in their shoes. You click the science fiction category and see the top 20 books. You automatically discount anything that doesn't draw your eye. If you're into giant spaceship stories, then your gaze is going to land on the books that have a giant spaceship.

We've already discussed mimicking other successful books in your genre, specifically self-published books. A big 5 publisher can slap almost any cover on a book and still get it to succeed. One of the first covers for *Jurassic Park* didn't even have a dinosaur. But we need to be a lot more sensitive to reader preferences.

When I selected my cover artist for *Destroyer* I contacted Nick Webb, and Joshua Dalzelle to ask who they used. Their books were kicking ass, and part of the reason why was their phenomenal covers. I settled on the artist Nick used, and I paid a pretty penny for the privilege. But you know what? I made up for that by paying less for editing, which I discussed in the last chapter. If I have to pick one thing that will sell the book, that's cover- not editing. So I splurged on the cover, and the result had me making this face =0

It's my hope that readers feel the same. The cover looks amazing as a thumbnail, and it looks even better at full size. If a reader lands on my product page, they'll be blown away by the cover. That's the first hurdle.

Title

Title is the next hurdle. It needs to speak to your target reader, to be easily understandable. Let's look at the ones I used when researching my military sci-fi experiment. *Constitution* and *Warship* are a single word. *The Lost Starship* is three. All three are about the ship on the cover, and most readers make that connection. For *Warship* and *The Lost Starship* that's apparent from the words chosen. *Constitution* is a little bit more of a stretch, but it also hits the right notes for the readers in the genre.

The original U.S.S. Constitution was one of the most famous naval vessels of all time. It was commissioned by George

Washington, and also had the nickname Old Ironsides. That fits astoundingly well with the plot of the book, and readers who get the connection are much more likely to buy the book. Readers who don't can still associate the single word title with the glorious ship on the cover. Win-win.

So what did I take from this? I named my book *Destroyer*. Before doing so I perused Amazon to see if there were any other novels with the same title. There is one, but it's in a totally different genre. Readers are very unlikely to confuse the two books.

Why *Destroyer*? It's a class of military vessel that every reader of military science fiction is immediately familiar with. If you're a reader who isn't familiar with that lore, the title still has some punch. It's clearly about the, wait for it, destroyer on the cover of my book.

As mentioned above, the title needs to resonate with the reader. Look at the title of the book you're reading. *Write to Market* makes it immediately clear what you're going to learn, just like *5,000 Words Per Hour*. Titles are critical. Choose them with care.

Blurb

The next cornerstone of your book's packaging is the blurb. This one is a real doozy too, because copywriting is a very difficult skill to master. Your blurb needs to grab the reader in the first sentence, and it needs to have them fully hooked by the third. It has to be short and punchy, but also inform the reader of exactly what type of story they're about to read. How do you do that? By describing the stakes, and mentioning the key tropes.

If you look at *Constitution*, *Warship*, and *The Lost Starship* all of them mention their maverick captain. All of them mention mankind being ill prepared for the war that is about to come. All of them mention that one ship is mankind's only hope. Guess what my blurb is going to sound like?

I will hit all the same notes, but change up the blurb to be specific to my plot. I want to appeal to the same readers. Remember, you want familiar, but unique. If you read *Dead Man*'s blurb it's clear the book isn't the Dresden Files, but if you liked the Dresden Files, you'll quickly realize it has the same elements. *Dead Man* is about a Black Magic Outlaw. Those three words convey a ton of meaning, just like Wizard Private Investigator. You can easily spot the connection.

Blurbs are difficult to get right, but thankfully you have

a wonderful tool. The blurbs of every successful book you seek to emulate. You can't copy, but you can look for trends just like you have in every other part of writing to market.

Look Inside

This is your last line of defense, the thing that will separate the *Hunger Games* clone from a hit that will compete with it. At the end of the day your packaging will only go so far, and everything will come down to the writing. If you want to succeed at this game, then you need to write a compelling novel that hits the tropes readers are after.

Amazon's Look Inside feature allows readers to peruse the first several chapters before they buy. Even people who buy before reading the look inside are going to know within a few chapters whether or not they want to continue, so you need to hook them fast. Your first few chapters need to be incredible, or readers will drop your book and move on.

So how do you do that? First, you need to appeal to the meat of the genre. In the case of *No Such Thing As Werewolves* I had a gigantic, technologically impossible pyramid push its way

out of the earth in the mountains of Peru. A team of soldiers
was there to meet it, though they had no idea how their employer
could possibly have known the pyramid was going to arrive. They
investigate, only to encounter a werewolf that was evidently
waiting inside. By the end of that first chapter several people
are dead, and people are left wondering what the pyramid is, why
there was a werewolf inside, and who sent the soldiers there.

What are the first chapters of the books you've studied
like?

Exercise #9- It's time to prep your book. Before you write
the very first word you want to know what you're going to write.
The easiest way to do that is to come up with the title and
blurb first. To that end, write out a list of 5 potential
titles. Write out a three paragraph blurb, and try to make it
sound as much like the blurbs of the books you studied as
possible. It's okay if neither the titles nor blurbs are
perfect. You're creating a starting point, and can continuously
refine them as you write the book.

Bonus: Commission or design a cover similar to the best
sellers in your genre. If budget is an issue, you can use a pre-

made cover, so long as it is the same quality as the other covers in your genre.

Chapter 10- Measuring Your Launch

Earlier in the book I talked about the launch of my first spin off series. *Hero Born* didn't perform as expected, and I realized almost immediately that I'd missed the mark. By the end of the first week I was certain, and the second week confirmed what I'd already known. The book had failed.

Many authors will argue that you can't know that quickly, that you need to give a book time. They'll point to books that sat quietly for months, or even years, then had a sudden resurgence of popularity. What those authors are ignoring is that most books that fail never have that resurgence. If your launch goes poorly, then odds are good you missed the mark.

So how do you know that, and more importantly what do you do about it?

Self-sustaining

Depending on genre, a successful launch could get you into the top #100 of the entire Amazon store, or it might stabilize around #15,000. Either is fine depending on the level of success you're after, nor does a specific rank tell you anything by itself. When I realized *Hero Born* had failed it was still ranked at #10,000 in the store, something many authors would love to have.

I knew it had failed, because it was *trending downward*. By that I mean that day after day its rank was lower. Sometimes it would spike up a little, but overall it sank. If you hit the mark, if your book has the right tropes, and hits the right notes, then it will find a natural equilibrium. For *No Such Thing As Werewolves* that equilibrium was around the #4,000 mark. With no promotion from me it sold around the same number of copies every day, all off the back of organic discovery.

Part of that is also bought books, but a large part of it is Amazon showing your book to people who might like it. That's where the real magic happens, and where it was missing with *Hero Born*. If the almighty Zon shows your book to a batch of people, and very few buy it, then they'll stop showing it to people. If, on the other hand, they show it to people and people *do* buy it, then Amazon will keep showing it.

At the end of the day Amazon exists to sell products. They're very, very good at studying reader habits, and realize very quickly whether or not any given book will play to a specific market. If you write your book to market, and have the right packaging, you stand a high chance of Amazon peddling it for you.

Your book will become self-sustaining, and its success will be enhanced by any promotion you add. But if you're lacking that initial self-sustaining quality no amount of promotion will save your book. You'll move copies when you run sales, and you may get mailing list subscribers to buy it, but you're not going to thrive through organic discovery.

Reacting Quickly

So what do you do if you launch your book, and it falls flat like *Hero Born*? You run the same sort of analysis you did on the best selling books in your genre. Theirs succeeded, and yours didn't. Why? Did you miss the mark with tropes? Was your cover not up to snuff? How about your blurb? Or, and this can most definitely happen, did the market change? Reader tastes are constantly evolving, and it's very possible the genre that was hot when you started has since cooled.

Finding the answer to these difficult questions can be very challenging. Start by conducting the exact same analysis you did before. Are the books you emulated still selling well? Look at your cover next to theirs. Be honest. Does it measure up? Does it hit the same notes? What are the tropes they're using in their blurbs? Are you using them too?

Hopefully you can figure out where you went wrong, but whether you can or can't your response should be exactly the same. Research your next book. If this launch was successful, then start on the sequel. If it wasn't, either write another book in that genre, or move to another genre. If you wrote under a pen name, this is easy. Simply make another pen name.

When I realized that *Hero Born* had failed I was in a difficult position. I'd already started writing *Hero Rising*, the sequel. Worse, I'd listed a pre-order on Amazon. If I decided to cut bait Amazon would ban me from pre-orders for a year. I'd also upset long time fans who expected the sequel. I wrote myself into a corner. Learn from my mistake. Don't commit to writing a full series until you're sure the first book will sell.

If that book doesn't sell, it's quite all right to cut bait and move on to another series. Time after time I've watched authors labor on a series that wasn't selling. They struggle to get books out, because their enthusiasm has waned. They know it won't sell, and that's disheartening. But they do it anyway out of misplaced loyalty to the reader.

I'm all for finishing series you start, but you also need to eat and pay rent. If a series crashes and burns, do what you have to do.

Exercise #10 - I found this exercise rather fun. Take a look at the Hot New Releases list for your category. Pick a book that you think will succeed, and then track that book for the next 30 days. Watch what it does. How does its rank change? If it succeeds, why do you think it did? What do the reviews say? If it fails, why do you think it missed the mark? What did it do wrong?

Bonus: Pick three books on the HNR list to track, and compare their success against each other. Odds are good at least one will succeed, and one will fail. Contrast the books and try to figure out why.

Chapter 11- Paying Your Dues

Domino Finn mentioned in a great post on Kboards that new writers have to pay their dues. What he meant is that in order to become successful, we need to build a readership. The easiest way to do that is by writing to market. If you put out great books that are similar to books people already like, then you are much more likely to sell copies.

Over time you'll build a larger mailing list. More and more people will know who you are. Once you reach critical mass, you can experiment and write the fun series that don't conform to the dominant tropes in your genre.

For now, though, the smart way to build sustainable success is to write to market. Pay your dues, and the freedom to write what you want will come.

Master Your Craft

There's another massive advantage in writing to market. The more closely you adhere to tropes, the more popular your book is likely to be. The more popular your book is, the more reader feedback you receive. That reader feedback teaches you valuable lessons. Did you mess up on dialogue? Did you have a character whose motivation wasn't clear?

We all have flaws in our writing, and no one is as good at catching them as passionate readers. The more books you write to market, the more you'll improve. The stronger your craft will become.

I suspect a fair number of readers want to write their magnum opus. For many of us, that's an epic fantasy series like The Wheel of Time, or Game of Thrones. I've lost count of the number of writer friends who've decided to write just such an epic.

They don't begin by writing a simple 60k word book with a beginning, middle, and end. No, they begin with their massive 12 volume epic. They do this despite the fact that they've never finished so much as a single novel. They've never practiced the nuances of character arc, plot, setting, or the myriad other skills we have to weave together as authors.

Every last one of those authors has failed to produce the quality of epic they wanted, and I am no exception. I have four separate attempts all trying to write my Shattered Gods fantasy epic. I failed, because my skills weren't up to snuff. They're still not up to snuff.

I've improved immensely over the last two years, because I've written nine books. I'll improve even more as I crank out another 12 this year. Every last one will teach me something, especially the ones I write to market.

Once I've paid my dues, once I've written twenty books, then and only then will I embark on that fantasy epic. I'll have a readership, and I'll have the skill to write the books I have dreamed about since I was a little kid. Patience and practice are what will get me there.

This more than anything else is why I urge you to try writing to market. Write the things you can achieve right now, and then learn from both your successes and failures. Accept that this is a career, and it will be years before you're producing your best work. There's no need to rush. Just take one step at a time, and you will get there.

A Note About Not Selling Out

If you've made it this far I'm hoping you now believe that writing to market isn't selling out, and can see the benefits of doing so. I want to warn you that you will be in the minority of writers, and you will suffer a lot of pushback from those who still believe you're selling out.

Most of those people will never read this book. They will not listen if you try to explain what writing to market really means. They believe they already know, and will react hostilely no matter what you try to do to persuade them.

If you're reading this a year or more after it has released I guarantee you there will be dozens of one star reviews. Many of those reviews are probably from people who didn't even read the book. The very idea of writing to market is so inflammatory that they feel compelled to slam it. I know this, because I saw exactly the same thing happen with 5,000 Words Per Hour.

This is a controversial topic, and by writing this book I put a gigantic target on my forehead. I'm willing to do that, because I think it's the right thing to do. Learning about writing to market is helping me make a living as an author, and since you've made it this far I think it can help you in exactly the same way.

I just want to warn you that you will meet resistance from other authors, especially if you start achieving the kind of success people like R.M. Webb and Cady Vance have. Be ready for that pushback, and if you don't like the sound of it, then consider keeping your pen name private.

Finally, I have a request. This book will ignite a firestorm. If you find the information helpful, please consider leaving a review. You're an author and know how important those are, and they'll be more important for this book than any other I've written.

Where do you go from here?

Now that you've finished this book it's time to start the real work. If you haven't already done the exercises in each chapter, then it's time. Turn the page, and start doing the work necessary to achieve the level of success you've always dreamed of. It's there, waiting.

If you liked this book enough that you want to read future books (I have three more coming this year), then please sign up for the mailing list. Either way I want to thank you for sticking with me through the entire book.

I hope it's been helpful, and I look forward to seeing you conquer the best seller lists!

-Chris

Exercises

Exercise #1- Find your Market

Write down the top three genres you enjoy writing in. It doesn't matter what those genres are, as long as you find them fun and interesting. Now open up www.amazon.com and browse the top selling books in each of those categories. What commonalties do you see between them? Women wielding magic? Giant spaceships? Down on their luck P.I.s? Click on the #1 book, and the #20 book in each category, and jot down that book's rank.

Which of these areas do you think you'd most enjoy writing? Scroll through the top #100 books in your chosen genre. Ideally the books on the last two pages should have ranks higher than #25,000. If they do, then congratulations, you have found the right intersection.

Exercise #2- Pick your favorite book or movie, the one you've seen / read countless times. Write out a list of ten tropes. These should be tropes you've seen in other books and movies. For example, Star Wars employs tropes like Chosen One, and Kindly Mentor. What other ones can you identify?

Exercise #3- Pick Books to Emulate

Go to Amazon and examine the top #20 books in your genre. Which ones are indie published? What is their ranking? How many reviews do they have? How long have they been out? Most importantly, how many books did the author publish in that genre before the book you're looking at took off?

Repeat this process until you have three books to use as case studies. We'll examine those books in depth in the next section.

Bonus: Spend time perusing the Also Bought books for each of the books you select. What commonalities do you see between covers and titles?

Exercise #4- This one is a doozy. Pick one of the books you researched in the last chapter. Read it, and as you're reading jot down notes on the tropes you see used. What's working in the book? What isn't? What makes this book similar to others in the genre, and how could you use the same tropes in new ways?

Bonus: Repeat this process for two more books.

Exercise #5- This is another tough one, because this is the longest chapter in the book. Pick one of the books from your list. Read the top 5 negative reviews, and the top 5 positive. What trends are you spotting? What did more than one reader like or dislike? Why do you think that is? Do these reviews give you some idea of who your target reader should be? If you're unsure, then take a look at a few of the reader profiles. What books did they like / dislike? For the one star reviews why do you feel their expectations weren't met? Why were they met for the 5 star reviews?

Bonus: Repeat this process for each of the three books you selected. I know that this is time consuming, but this is one of the most critical exercises in the book. Investing time here will be immensely useful later.

Exercise #6 - This was the hardest exercise in the book for me. If you've already completed and / or published a novel I want you to take a hard look at it now. Did it sell the way you wanted it to? If it did not, then ask yourself why? Did you violate reader expectations, and if so how? What genre were you aiming for, and how does your book differ from the books in that genre?

Write out a bulleted list with the answers.

Exercise #7 - It's time to set your goals. Take a hard look at how long it took to write your last novel. Use that time frame to extrapolate how long it will take to write the next one. Can you do it a little faster? Pick a date. Write that date down on a sticky note and put it on your monitor with the title of the book you want to finish.

Also add that date to your calendar, and add a reminder one

month from now that you're going to have the book done by then.

Bonus: Tell at least one friend about your goal. Accountability helps far, far more than people assume.

Exercise #8 - Get out a pad of paper, or open a blank document in your word processor of choice. Write down each distinct part of your writing business. Everything from writing, to plotting, to reading books on craft, to updating your website, to chatting with other authors. Rate each of these activities from 1 to 10, with 10 contributing the most to your success as an author. This should make it immediately clear what's important, and what's not.

How much faster could you write if you cut out everything 6 or below, and outsourced your 7 and 8s to a virtual assistant? What if you focused 100% of your time on the 9s and 10s? What would your author business look like?

Bonus: Brainstorm a pen name for the first novel you write to market.

Exercise #9- It's time to prep your book. Before you write the very first word you want to know what you're going to write. The easiest way to do that is to come up with the title and blurb first. To that end, write out a list of 5 potential titles. Write out a three paragraph blurb, and try to make it sound as much like the blurbs of the books you studied as possible. It's okay if neither the titles nor blurbs are perfect. You're creating a starting point, and can continuously refine them as you write the book.

Bonus: Commission or design a cover similar to the best sellers in your genre. If budget is an issue, you can use a pre-made cover, so long as it is the same quality as the other covers in your genre.

Exercise #10 - I found this exercise rather fun. Take a look at the Hot New Releases list for your category. Pick a book that you think will succeed, and then track that book for the next 30 days. Watch what it does. How does its rank change? If

it succeeds, why do you think it did? What do the reviews say?
If it fails, why do you think it missed the mark? What did it do
wrong?

Bonus: Pick three books on the HNR list to track, and
compare their success against each other. Odds are good at least
one will succeed, and one will fail. Contrast the books and try
to figure out why.

34563631R00059

Made in the USA
Middletown, DE
25 August 2016